Nicholas Murray

A QUARTET IN WINTER

Rack Press

First published in a limited edition of 150 copies,
the first fifty numbered and signed by the author.

Note: p6, 'Sais' in Welsh means 'Englishman' and 'sans-papiers' in French means an illegal immigrant without identification papers; p10, 'und so weiter' in German means 'and so on'.

Published in Wales by Rack Press,
The Rack, Kinnerton, Presteigne, Powys, LD8 2PF
Tel: 01547 560 411
All orders and correspondence: rackpress@nicholasmurray.co.uk

ISBN 978-1-8382303-0-2

Printed by Artisan Print, Presteigne, Powys

Sing us no more idylls, no more pastorals,
  No more epics of the English earth;
The country is a dwindling annexe of the factory...
          Louis MacNeice, *Autumn Journal*

ONE

Autumn is ending, the last leaves scamper on the lane,
and frost lays its dust-sheet on the Radnor hills.
I look towards England through a misted pane
and note how garish sun gilds the black sills.

The usual thoughts in border country: here in Wales
we are like you, hikers in red socks on Hergest Ridge.
On Ordnance maps the tyranny of dotted lines prevails,
but in a world of hedge and wire: nothing we can't bridge.

A squirrel walks the high wire from post to post,
our email traffic under her toes, her balancing a feat
deserving loud applause, but there are urgencies of toast
and smoking coffee – until a need that brings us to our feet

to climb the stair again, enter the study's bookish peace,
rows of stacked volumes padding the monkish cell
and the lamp lit on a dull morning, a zipped-up fleece
aiding the two-bar fire: all preparations to *write well:*

I'd be so lucky! pulling down a book of verse to prod
my morning efforts into something like a hopeful riff,
in which an image comes unsought, as inspiration should,
not artificial, *voulu*, its bones unsupple, arthritic, stiff.

Should poets write in steady verse, filling the old forms
with newer wine, offering the pleasure of a clinching rhyme?
Or break new ground, *disrupt* like tech-firm giants, all the norms
that keep us where we are (or were) *viz.* the primeval slime

rather than showing the glint of Heaven's gate
in scintillating shapes that force the language to new ways
of being? Or both? Like Eliot, whose skill could innovate
to startle, or warm us with a witty, playful phrase?

These thoughts arrive to slow the serious start of work.
I'm expert in the stratagems of sly delay,
skilled in the tricks devised to dodge and shirk
the task of getting down to it, broaching the new day.

Outside, the freezing fog is pushing down to stifle
the joyful zest that should precede creation.
What's more this must appear a playful trifle
when so much vexes and dismays the nation:

pandemic, poverty, the mattering of black lives,
the wicked slaver's statue tumbled in a dock,
young people dying from a hateful trade in knives,
the Earth in agony as we deplete its stock.

O, don't be such a misery! Disperse that mist! Rejoice!
It's early winter, snowfall hasn't yet filled up the lanes,
the frost makes pretty patterns, and the robin's voice
brightens the day, however cold, however hard it rains.

Two

Morning in Wales; our cottage on the hill; its famous view.
Frankly, three decades on, how could anyone be happier?
Though a migrant, incomer, monoglot (insults: form a queue)
I live here in the lovely Marches (*Sais! Sans-papiers!*).

Two worker's cottages knocked into one (before our time),
look out on buzzards or the swooping kite
Placed on our shelf of land (did I say?) the view's sublime
in every season, but in glittering snow-time pure delight.

That's it: smugly and snugly in a cottage 'meant for two'
(like Daisy's tandem in the song) we're asking to be told:
you must remember that not everyone's like you;
spare a thought for the homeless, out in the pitiless cold.

I can't dissent; too few are lucky, too many have it tough.
The ten per cent own ninety of the wealth, the shits!
If I could wave a wand (or pay more tax) then, fair enough,
I'd do it now – though in my case the hair shirt never fits

so *make* me do it, will you, in a way that works; remind me
each time to write a cheque or say: I'm sorry
that the people in the lengthening queue behind me
at Lidl can't afford to wait in for the Waitrose lorry.

They call this Virtue Signalling, so bring on Vice,
Bring on Attila, horrible Hun; Adolf, tweet!
Let us be nasty; how I hate the Nice,
the 'liberal elites' who strut along the street,

heads in the air, full of fine phrases,
callous to the 'left behind' in Northern cities.
Bring on the cops with cuffs and tasers;
send back the migrants no one pities.

Hate's far more true than love and Number One
is where it's at, not cold abstractions like Society
(a fig leaf to prevent us getting on:
you po-faced devotees of Puritan propriety).

I don't believe that stuff, nor you, I think,
but standing here, under a winter sky of grey,
I feel an inner chill; my heart begins to sink
faced with a future that looks darker by the day.

Can't we do better? Are the iron men the way?
In rasping comments, backed by force,
pretending to befriend the working class, they say
that liberal democracy has had its day

and their strong arms alone can keep the peace:
the whistling drone, the cluster bomb, their means
to crush dissent abroad, while back at home they fleece
their people, smirking kleptocrats on giant screens

that show them shaking hands with fellow-crooks,
investor, asset-stripper, fly consultant, gnome
who teach them all the ways to cook the books,
put in a bill, then take the first flight home.

Money's loquacious, power corrodes – old clichés never die
but are reborn across the tracts of time; can't we resist,
by saying no, simply refusing every long-spun lie
that power tells (its emphasis the knuckle-dustered fist)?

THREE

A hare comes lolloping along the lane,
preferring asphalt to the furrowed fields
on which small tracks indent the snow, and yellow stain
of urine from some creature or the rut of wheels

dissolve the purity of driven snow that lies
in layers on each branch and thorn,
catching the sunlight that has slit the skies
to lift that heavy mist that hung since dawn.

Seeing my stare, it rises to full height then leaps
into a shake of snowy growth, its instinct sure
to find the safety it knows: the company it keeps,
in its own lightly-covered form, secure.

After this meeting which is fine and rare
the morning alters, sounds a different note.
I call to mind the *Shepherd's Calendar* of Clare
or Richard Jefferies: observers from a world remote

from our millennial, agri-business countryside
where great machines, banana-coloured, grind
along small lanes, their massive wheels so wide
I marvel at the space they always seem to find

through which to squeeze themselves, then roar,
triumphant like a chariot or juggernaut.
Sheep merely chew and in their placid fields ignore
the racket that such engines generate.

The countryside's a noisy place of barking dogs
and shouts and chain-saws screaming
so slip inside and watch the glowing logs
in the ingle-nook while softly dreaming

of summer days, of post-pandemic trips,
when we are free again to roam a little wider
(much as we love our patch, the waves and quips
of neighbours in their passing trucks: *und so weiter*).

However strong the ties that bind one to this place,
we're wanderers (Chatwin said) who sicken
when penned inside; we need to up and chase
some moving quarry lest mental arteries thicken.

Throw something in a bag, get on the road,
travel light, with open plans not Google Maps,
which bossily impose the one right way and goad
us to adopt *their* route, *their* A to B, seductive traps

that wipe out serendipity, the freedom of the trail
that winds its own way at its chosen speed.
Ignore the vile *required fields* on your form. Set sail
when the wind rises, don't do as the Guide decreed.

FOUR

December's here and winter takes command,
we meekly follow what it says, and brace for colder nights,
fresh snow blown in curvaceous shapes, the frozen land
hard under our boots, then after 4 switch on the lights.

That's without Jan and Feb whose bag of tricks
is being packed: short days, long nights, dull skies.
The summerhouse locked up, another door that sticks
until the summer warms its pores, heaps of dead flies

in toolshed corners, skeleton trees bare as fence stakes,
black mould's slow creep on cold stone walls,
the unused spades and hoes and rakes –
O make us warm and dry again, unthaw our souls.

But wait! soon the green spikes of snowdrop tips
arrive, minutely, in the little wood; all is not lost.
Then Christmas with its pardonable *kitsch*,
repels the cheerless antics of persistent frost.

The Earth we treat so roughly has its own designs,
happy to sleep through winter months and rest
before its sends us its auspicious signs
of growth, renewal, spurt of pent-up zest.

Just think if seasons didn't hold their grip
what would we moan about while waiting for the bus?
Like owlish dons, hair-splitting in their scholarship,
our tracing of each weather-shift's our syllabus,

our post-grad course, the thing we know,
our creed, our science, our pagan fetish.
Like Eskimos with countless words for snow,
our constant talk of weather makes us British.

East Radnor, November-December 2020